How To Be The Almost

Perfect Husband

By Wives Who Know

ALSO COMPILED BY J.S. SALT

How To Be The Almost Perfect Wife
By Husbands Who Know

Always Kiss Me Good Night
Instructions on Raising the Perfect Parent
By 147 Kids Who Know

Always Accept Me for Who I Am
Instructions from Teenagers
on Raising the Perfect Parent

How To Be The Almost
Perfect Husband

By Wives Who Know

COMPILED BY J. S. SALT

To all my contributors

~

Published by
Shake It! Books
P.O. Box 6565
Thousand Oaks, CA 91359
Toll Free: (877) Shake It
www.**shake**that**brain**.com

This book is available at special discounts for bulk purchase for sales promotions, premiums, fund-raising and educational use.
Special books, or book excerpts, can also be created to fit specific needs.

ISBN: 0-9667156-1-6
10 9 8 7 6 5 4 3 2 1
First Edition

One advantage of marriage . . .
is that when you fall out of love with him
or he falls out of love with you,
it keeps you together
until you maybe fall in again.

—JUDITH VIORST

Contents

Introduction

If you could tell someone how to be the almost perfect husband, what would you tell him?

That's the question I posed to more than one thousand wives, ex-wives and widows, nearly all of whom freely offered advice. The result is a collection of outstanding *insider's advice*—so husbands can learn what their wives truly crave; and wives, at the very least, can point and say: *See, that's what I need. Just like this wife says on page _____.*

Guaranteed. The book you now hold in your hands will serve as *a catalyst for conversation*, leading you and your spouse to better understanding...and a better marriage.

Or give this insider's guide, and its companion volume, *How to Be the Almost Perfect Wife—By Husbands Who Know*, to a couple that's *about* to get married.

These small but important books will surely improve any union or marriage. They've even improved my own marriage. (And it was pretty good *before* the books.)

J.S. SALT

Communication

*Share your thoughts
and fears,
and let me do the same.*

—LESLIE, 51
married 30 years

Always listen to what your wife has to say no matter how uninteresting or boring it is to you—it's important to her or she wouldn't be sharing it with you.

—BARBARA, 36
married 12 years
"known hubby 25 years"

When I'm having a bad day and complaining a lot, please just listen. Forget the advice on how to make things better.
Just tell me you love me and give me a hug.

—BECKY, 33
married 12 years

I know you want to help, but please
don't jump in with a solution before
I've finished telling you my problem.
Sometimes all I need is a sympathetic ear.

—LINDA, 40
married 15½ years

Call me during the day to let me know
you're thinking about me.
It's a little thing . . . but it means a lot.

—Victoria, 30+

It's not enough to "talk" to me by e-mail.
During the day, I need to hear
your voice now and then.

—Jessica, 27
married 2 1/2 years

Ask her how she's feeling
and listen with your heart
(not just your head).

—MAGGIE, 42
2nd marriage of 12 years

8

Always call home when you're going
to be late. That way she won't
worry about you—*or get angry with you.*

—PHYLLIS, 42
married 21 years

9

Think before you speak.
Words can damage and
cut to the bone.

—JEANNIE, 55
married 22 years, separated 7 years

For every negative statement,
say at least a dozen positive things.
Maybe it's my fragile self-esteem,
but what you think and say about me
colors so much how I see myself.
So please be selective in what you say.

—JEANETTA
married 2 years

When you are upset with me or the kids, sit down with me and *explain* what's bothering you. Don't hide your emotions or pound out your frustrations in the garage. Come and talk things out with me—so I can understand your point of view.

—ANN, 65
divorced after 26 years

When you're angry,
tell your wife why.
Don't say,
"If you don't know,
I'm not going to tell you."

—PAMELA, 53
2nd marriage of 6 years

Please do not raise your voice in anger.

—CATHIE, 47
married 25 years

You'll never win me over through
shouting or yelling. The louder you get,
the less I hear. *(Whisper sweet nothings,
however, and I'll follow you anywhere.)*

—SUE, 41
married 5 years

Don't just say,
"That's how I am."
You wouldn't accept it
from the children
and I won't accept it
from you.

—KAREN, 46
3rd marriage of 6 years

Before you blow up—*well before!*—
ask yourself just how important
this issue will be two weeks from
now . . . a month . . . a year . . .
a lifetime.

—FRAN, 55
married 33 years

16

PLEASE, PLEASE don't end an argument
by telling me I'm stupid, callous and
don't understand anything, followed by
"Okay, let's go to bed."
If you can, arrange the accidental touch
when we've gone to bed angry. Making love
is a great way to put the fight behind us.

—MAUREEN, 62
married 42 years

17

Give up faultfinding and blame.

—FRAN, 43
divorced

Apologize when
you're wrong.
Forgive when you're not.

—JAN, 42
3rd marriage of 1¹/₂ years

We don't need to agree all the time.
But when we don't agree, I need you to try
to understand and *respect* my position.

—GAIL, 38
married 14 years

Even if you don't think I *should* feel a certain way, at least try to understand *why* I'm feeling that way.

—MARY, 55
2nd marriage of 10 years

When I'm trying to talk with you
I need you to stop what you're doing and look me
in the eye—so I know you're really listening.

—MADDIE, 43
married 2 years

Your eyes are on mine but your mind is elsewhere.
Please, oh, please, LISTEN when I talk.

—RUTH, 68
married 48 years

It makes me lonely when you speak to me over your shoulder or from behind the newspaper. Really look at me, right into my eyes at least twice a day. It doesn't matter what the topic is: It's the connection that counts.

—SHIRLEY, 41
divorced

Before marriage, a man declares that he would lay down his life to serve you; after marriage, he won't even lay down his newspaper to talk to you.

—HELEN ROWLAND

Tell your wife constantly
that she is the best thing
that ever happened to you.
This will help to remind
you as well.

—SALLY, 55
married 3 years

Love & Affection

Instead of just telling me, *show* me
you love me. A kiss when I least expect it.
Flowers for no reason. Hold my hand
when we're in public, and in private.
Little surprises like these can sometimes
mean much more than words.

—JENNIFER, 22
married 9 months

Write me little notes and give me
funny cards a little more often,
like you did when we were
"courting." (I've kept every letter
and note you ever sent me.)

—JENNIFER, 32
married 6 years

Once in a while, send me a little surprise at work—so the people around me are jealous that I have the perfect mate.

—MARILEE, 46
married 22 years

Surprise her with something small
but important, like bringing home
take-out without being asked.

—ROWENA, 46
married 23 years

It's the day-to-day things he does that count: filling my water glass when it's empty, giving me the best steak off the grill, getting up on a cold night to get me an aspirin and a glass of water.

—ANNA, 52
"married 35 years ago at age 17"

The little things you do for me mean much more to me than lavish presents on special occasions.

—LYNDA, 50
married 22 years

When you go to bed before I do, turn down my side of the bed as well. And don't forget to turn on the night light. It makes me feel taken care of.

—MADDIE, 43
married 2 years

Get me out of bed in the morning.
Take responsibility for me starting my day.
(Even better, start with sex.)

—PAULA, 41
married 12 years

If we're both awake when you get out of bed, be sure to give me a little kiss. If we don't connect when we first wake up, I'm more likely to get irritated with you about little things throughout the day.

—DEBORAH, 42
married 5 years

Always kiss me
good morning and good night.

—PENNY, 40 SOMETHING
2nd marriage of 15 years

Never leave the house
without a goodbye kiss.

—CATHIE, 28
divorced

When you roll over in the middle of the night (even when we are truly asleep) and whisper you love me . . .
I'll follow you anywhere.

—KAREN, 46
3rd marriage of 6 years

Do what my husband does: When I wake up at 3 A.M. filled with worry, he rubs my back, holds my hand and says things will look better in the light of day. Then he doesn't fall asleep until I do.

—CYNTHIA
married 14 years

Sometimes it was worth all the disadvantages of marriage just to have that: one friend in an indifferent world.

—ERICA JONG

Light a candle every once in a while
—even when the power doesn't go out.

—LINDA, 48
married 28 years

Remember you're my lover,
not just a friend. Let's have less chatter
about mundane household chores
and more playfulness, tender
endearments and romantic tension.
Otherwise, our lovemaking seems
like a weary obligation.

—PAM, 37
married 9 years

No more quickies!
(Well, maybe occasionally is okay.)
And be more adventurous:
like cooking together
with only aprons.

—NANCI, 55
married 3 years

Don't touch me only when you want to have sex. Touch me in little ways throughout the day. That way, I feel connected to you and I want to make love. Not as something separate, but as a *continuance* of my connection to you. In other words... more non-sexual touching more often will get you more *sexual* touching more often.

—STACY, 32
married 12 years

Please! Put your teeth in your mouth
before you kiss me.
I'd rather be bitten than gummed!

—ALYSON, 68
married 23 years

Tell her she looks pretty.
Often.

—Deborah, 42
married 5 years

Look at me—really—before
you say I look great.

—Phyllis, 55
married 25 years

When asked, "How do I look?"
feign careful study
and awestruck admiration.

—SARA, 38
married 20 years

When she looks in the mirror and
HOWLS at the rate at which
gravity is reshaping her jaw line
DON'T offer to buy her a face lift.
All she needs to hear is
"Honey, I love your face."

—KATE
divorced after 23 years

*Remind me that stretch marks aren't ugly,
but are instead visible proof that I brought
three perfect lives into the world.*

—TRACI
married 7 years

Never mention fat.

—PEGGY, 47

Take time out to compliment me.
It means a lot to me to know you noticed.

—KARIN, 39
married 15 years

Even though I'm strong and
modern and self-sufficient,
do surprising, sweet, I'm-here-to-
pamper-and-care-for-you things.

—ERIKA, 45
married 15 years

Recognize that inside this confident,
in-control woman is a child
who needs your love and comfort.

—SHIRLEY, 61
married 35 years

When I am at my most "prickly"
—when I am the least
approachable—is exactly
when I most need to be touched
and held. It will melt away
so much that is troubling me.

—CATE, 40

I love it when you insist
that I hug and kiss you even
when I'm in a really bad mood.
No matter what, I always feel better.

—JENNIFER, 32
married 6 years

Never stop courting, impressing me
and flirting with me like you did the
first time we met. My body may be aging,
but in my mind I'm still 18.

—LINDA, 40
married 15 years

On Valentine's Day don't ask our daughter if she'll be your Valentine.

—PAULA, 41
married 12 years

Hold her hand just because.

—DEBBIE

A lot more hugs, a lot more affection.
Life is a dance, not a battle of wills.

—JANET, 53
married 16 years, widowed

Learn to say "I love you"
—acting as if you do is great,
but it's nice to hear it once in a while.

—MAUREEN, 62
married 42 years

Tell her you love her 3 times a day.
"I love you" is like mayonnaise.
It has a very short shelf life.

—SALLY, 47

The almost perfect husband
(one of which I have) is kind.
That's it and that's enough.

—VICTORIA, 49
2nd marriage of 2 years

Home & Family

When you walk in the door,
kiss *ME* before you kiss the baby.

—MADDIE, 43
married 2 years

When you're here, *be* here.
Don't think about work or sports.
Focus on your wife and children.
They're talking to you
but you're not here.

—GENA, 36
married 7 years

Pay more attention to what's going on with the family. When you put your nose in the newspaper every second you have some down time, I feel ignored—like I'm shouldering all the household and child-rearing responsibilities.

—SHERRY, 43
married 16 years

Be more involved with the family. Help out with the kids and their school. And take *pleasure* in it.

—LESLIE, 36
married 8 years

Spend time
with your kids, now.
If you wait until Tomorrow . . .
it may be too late.

—TAMMY, 39

If you wind up the kids before bedtime,
you'd better be willing to put them to bed!

—GWEN, 39
married 8 years

Learn from my husband: He does the dishes while I'm putting the kids to bed. Then we *both* get the rest of the evening—to spend together or by ourselves. This does wonders for our marriage and my sanity.

—JUDY, 36
married 6 years

Ask her if you can pick up the kids
or run an errand for her—so
she can have some time for *herself*.

—MAGGIE, 42
2nd marriage of 12 years

Now and then, let her have a day to herself.
It's a wonderful gift that won't cost you a thing.

—SUZANNA, 43
married 15 years

I want to be alone. I just want to be alone.

—GRETA GARBO

Don't say "I'll help you" with jobs around the house. Realize that the house, the kids, the cat, the cars, the laundry, all of it are ours. Offer to take some of *our* jobs and do them.

—OLIVETTE, 44
married 13 years

Either do your share of the housework
or SMILE when you write a check
to the cleaning lady.

—PAMELA, 53
2nd marriage of 6 years

Whenever your wife prepares
a home-cooked meal,
let her know you *appreciate* the effort.

—PENE, 56
married 29 years

Never frown at the meatloaf.

—JULIA, 42

If you get home before I do take the initiative and prepare something for dinner. And don't just make macaroni for the kids and forget about us.

—LESLIE, 36
married 8 years

Every now and then,
cook dinner for your wife.
Getting taken out for dinner is
nice, but so is staying home
and being pampered with a meal.

—MAUREEN, 62
married 42 years

When life gets out of control, have a sense
of humor about it. After all, it's the things
you love most—the kids, me, our house—
that often send things out of control.

—ELENA, 37
married 11 years

Home repairs are a part of life.
When a doorknob falls off, please don't
react like the world is falling apart.

—AMY, 32
married 2 years

The perfect husband will stay calm and rational. When he gets lost, he will ask for directions. When he misplaces his keys, he will mentally retrace his steps and use reason to find them. He will not allow life's little frustrations to get the better of him and cause a crisis for his wife and family.

—MARY, 53
2nd marriage of 12 years

Daily: Be funny.

Weekly: Take out the garbage.

—JEAN, 42
"married 12 glorious years"

Support & Acceptance

Remember to tell your wife
—daily if you can—
how much you appreciate
all that she does.

—Victoria, 30+

Praise your wife
—even for the little things.

—SUSAN
married 28 years

Don't just tell others
how proud you are of me.
Tell ME!

—JUDY, 50 +
married 30 years

When you meet up with friends,
introduce me for heaven's sake.
I'm not a statue standing next to you!

—KATE
divorced after 23 years

Don't embarrass me or make fun of me
in front of other people.

—BARBARA, 68
married 49 years

Support me in public.
You can discuss
our *differences* in private.

—PENNY, "40 something"
2nd marriage of 15 years

Love me enough to help me reach
my goals. Don't hold me back because
you're afraid of losing me. Help me
be the dreamer you fell in love with.

—MARY, 29
married 12 years

You'll never know how much time
(psychologically, emotionally,
intellectually and physically)
it takes to raise a child and then
run a business. So try to focus on
the 999 things I get done,
not the 1 thing I don't.

—GAIL, 38
married 14 years

84

*Give her
the benefit of the doubt.*

—MIRIAM
married 25 years

When I say "Leave me alone"
at least try to figure out if I really
mean it or if I want to talk about
the problem. Sometimes
I don't know for sure myself.

—LINDA, 48
married 28 years

When I have an emotional
outburst, don't leave the room.
Care enough to sit there, BE
with me, and hold me when I cry.

—BETH, 31
married 5 years

In times of stress, please talk to me
in soothing terms—to help me
bring myself back into balance.

—GLORIA, 50
widow

Never try to control your wife. She has a brain of her own and can think independently of you. Controlling spouses see things in black and white. (*I'm right, so you must be wrong.*) In reality, neither spouse should give up their identity in a relationship; nor should they be asked to.

—MARSHA, 50
married 4 years ("after age 40!")

I'm not a foreign country to be conquered and dominated; I'm a path of endless variety to be explored and cherished.

—KANDY, 41
2nd marriage of 5 years

Let me do things *MY* way
—without telling me a better way—
which generally translates to *YOUR* way.

—Verna, 52
2nd marriage of 17 years

Treat your wife as if she were as smart as you.
(She is, you know.)

—Carol, 65

married 15 years

Don't try to convince me that my feelings are
not "rational" and therefore not valid.

—GAIL, 38
married 14 years

Respect my feelings. You don't have to agree
with them, but I have a right to feel the way I do.
I'm my own entity, not an extension of you.
And when I'm talking to you,
don't point the TV remote and click it at me!

—MARY KAY, 42
married 18 years

Appreciate your wife and cherish her for
herself—instead of comparing her
to some "ideal" in your head.

—JOAN, 67
married 26 years

Continue to look at
all my flaws
as charming little quirks.

—HESTER, 50
married 20 years

Never try to make me feel guilty about making bad financial decisions —especially when they're in the under $20 range.

—VICKI, 46
married 23 years

When we go to pick my mother up
at the airport, I want you to park
the car and go in to the gate with me
instead of circling the airport.

—MARGE, 46
married 23 years

Treat my mother
with loving kindness.

—PAT, 54
married 19 years

If you can remember someone's batting average 10 years later, you can learn to remember your own family's birthdays.

—WENDY, 43
2nd marriage of 3 years

> Marriage is the alliance of two people, one of whom never remembers birthdays and the other never forgets them.
>
> —OGDEN NASH

The perfect husband would notice
when his wife has dark smudges
beneath her eyes and insist that she rest.

—CARLA JEANNE, 49
married 22 years

Don't let your wife take on
more than she can handle.

—LESLIE, 51
married 30 years

When your wife seems stressed, ask her,
"What do you need from me right now?"

—SUSAN, 50

Don't wait until I ask for help.
Volunteer.

—LINDA, 48
married 28 years

Learn from my husband, a man who has stood by his wife following the loss of their premature baby daughter, a man who listened to a doctor tell them that their son had a rare genetic disease and they could very well lose him, a man who is a true hero in the sense that he doesn't run when the "going gets tough"— who is willing to accept that life isn't always fair & things don't always go as planned.

—STEPHANIE, 34
married 7 1/2 years

Us

Take her on a "date" at least once a week
—like *before* you got married.

—CHARLENE, 43
married 24 years

I look forward to date night all week. It keeps the
sparkle in the relationship. The longer you're married,
the more important date night is.

—MICHELLE PFEIFFER

I'll go to the ball game
if you go to the
symphony with me.

—HENRIETTA, 63
married 17 years

Let's go off on little weekend trips
by ourselves—so we can rediscover
why we fell in love, and what we found
special about each other.

—KARIN, 39
married 15 years

When you create time for just the two of us
it affirms to me that I am special to you.
You have to plan these times—they don't
just "happen." It can be as simple as
a bike ride or a trip to the ice cream store.
Either way, it tells me that the rest of the
world can wait—*your choice for this moment
is to be with me.*

—DENISE, 41
married 22 years "to my high school sweetheart!"

ALWAYS take a vacation—
just for the two of you—EVERY year:
to heal the soul, mend the heart,
and make new memories.

—SHERYL, 51
3rd marriage of 10 years
"third time is the charm"

What you do *with* me
is more important than what you do for me.
Our days are packed and sometimes
we shut the kids out because we're too "busy."
But I believe, in the end, our most cherished
moments will be when we...
-sat on the floor and played with the baby
-couldn't stop laughing
-acted silly
-made mistakes and didn't care
-didn't have a plan.

—CLAUDIA, 40
2nd marriage of 5 years

Be proud of yourself.
You do not need to prove
you are a man by being
more sexual, making more money
or being dominant.

—JUNE, 71
married 36 years, widowed

Lighten up. Allow yourself to make mistakes. You're loved for who you are, how you act—not for your "position in life" or your earning power. Be you! That's who I fell in love with.

—JENNIFER, 62
2nd marriage of 6 1/2 years

Don't become the person your
ambition wants
you to be and
forget everything else.

—KELLY, 32
divorced after 4 years

Don't withdraw.
By all means grab a "time out"
when you need it but don't let hours
become weeks.

—KATE
divorced after 23 years

As you get older, and your wife does too,
and you have to make decisions about
medical concerns and wills, and accompany
each other to doctor appointments, keep on
doing those impromptu, fun things you
used to do—a little dance in the kitchen,
a surprise gift, a pinch on the bottom.

—MARIE, 62
married 42 years

We need to laugh and have fun.
I *rely* on you to help me keep things
in perspective and not take ourselves
too seriously. Help me see
the "lighter side" in every situation.

—DENISE, 41
married 22 years "to my high school sweetheart!"

Treat your wife as you would
a best friend. Talk, joke, and
have fun with her. Tell her things
you've never told anyone else.
And when you're out with the guys,
call and tell her you miss her.

—CHRISTINE, 27
married 3 1/2 years

Treat your wife like a queen,
the most gorgeous woman on earth.

—ANN, 48
2nd marriage of 2 years

Treat me as if it's our last day together.

—CATHIE, 47
married 25 years

My Requests
(Notes to my husband)

My Requests
(Notes to my husband)

Volume II, Anyone?

 If you're a woman who's married, or used to be, you probably have your own instructions for *How To Be the Almost Perfect Husband*. Who knows? Your words could end up in *Volume II*. Just jot them down (including your name, age and vital statistics) and send them to:

J.S. Salt
c/o *Shake It! Books*
P.O. Box 6565
Thousand Oaks, CA 91359

Or e-mail your ideas to: wives@**shake**that**brain**.com

≈

And please include your mailing address. After all, if there is a *Volume II*—and we use your material—we'd like to send you a free autographed copy as our way of saying thanks.